THE NEW YORK RANGERS

CHERYL STRICKLER

Published by The Child's World®
800-599-READ • www.childsworld.com

Photography Credits
Cover: ©Chris Tanouye/Getty Images; page 5: ©Michael Mooney/NHLI/Getty Images; page 6: ©New York Times Co/Archive Photos/Getty Images; page 9: ©Steve Babineau/NHLI/Getty Images; page 10: ©Joshua Sarner/Icon Sportswire/Getty Images; page 12: ©Joshua Sarner/Icon Sportswire/Getty Images; page 12: ©Andrew Mordzynski/Icon Sportswire/Getty Images; page 13: ©Jared Silber/NHLI/Getty Images; page 13: ©Bruce Bennett Studios/Getty Images Studios/Getty Images; page 14: ©Jared Silber/NHLI/Getty Images; page 16: ©Jim McIsaac/Getty Images; page 16: ©Mitchell Layton/NHLI/Getty Images; page 17: ©Steve Crandall/Getty Images; page 17: ©Bruce Bennett Studios/Getty Images Studios/Getty Images; page 18: ©Focus on Sport/Getty Images; page 18: ©Bruce Bennett Studios/Getty Images Studios/Getty Images; page 19: ©J Giamundo/Bruce Bennett Studios/Getty Images Studios/Getty Images; page 19: ©Patrick McDermott/NHLI/Getty Images: page 20: ©Minas Panagiotakis/Getty Images Sport/Getty Images; page 20: ©Minas Panagiotakis/Getty Images Sport/Getty Images; page 21: ©Matthew Stockman/Getty Images; page 21: ©Minas Panagiotakis/Getty Images Sport/Getty Images; page 22: ©Jim McIsaac/Bruce Bennett/Getty Images; page 23: ©Bruce Bennett Studios/Getty Images Studios/Getty Images; page 25: ©J Giamundo/Bruce Bennett Studios/Getty Images Studios/Getty Images; page 26: ©Mark LoMoglio/NHLI/Getty Images; page 29: ©Steve Babineau/NHLI/Getty Images

ISBN Information
9781503870734 (Reinforced Library Binding)
9781503871939 (Portable Document Format)
9781503873179 (Online Multi-user eBook)
9781503874411 (Electronic Publication)

LCCN
2024950384

Printed in the United States of America

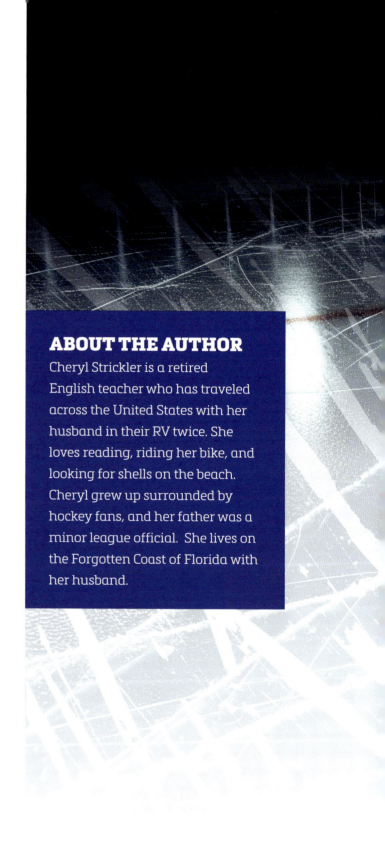

ABOUT THE AUTHOR

Cheryl Strickler is a retired English teacher who has traveled across the United States with her husband in their RV twice. She loves reading, riding her bike, and looking for shells on the beach. Cheryl grew up surrounded by hockey fans, and her father was a minor league official. She lives on the Forgotten Coast of Florida with her husband.

CONTENTS

Go Rangers!

The New York Rangers are a professional hockey team that plays in the National Hockey League (NHL). They play in the Metropolitan **Division** of the Eastern Conference. The Rangers have made the **playoffs** 63 times. The team won the Stanley Cup in their second season, becoming the first NHL team in the United States to do so. After winning the Stanley Cup in 1928, 1933, and 1940, it would be more than 50 years before the Rangers won another Stanley Cup in 1994.

Eastern Conference • Metropolitan Division

Carolina Hurricanes	New Jersey Devils	New York Rangers	Pittsburgh Penguins
Columbus Blue Jackets	New York Islanders	Philadelphia Flyers	Washington Capitals

Chris Kreider celebrates a goal with his teammates during a 2024 game.

Les Patrick (fourth from left) coached the Rangers for their first 13 seasons and led them to two Stanley Cup victories.

Becoming the Rangers

The Rangers are one of the original six teams of the NHL. The other five teams are the Boston Bruins, the Chicago Blackhawks, the Detroit Red Wings, the Montreal Canadiens, and the Toronto Maple Leafs. George "Tex" Rickard founded the Rangers in 1926. When the NHL first began, there were only four teams, and they were all Canadian. In 1924, the NHL decided to allow teams from the United States to join the league. The Original Six era ended in 1967 when the NHL added six **expansion teams** and doubled the size of the league. The Rangers' colors are blue, red, and white. The Rangers' logo has changed very little over the years, with the word *Rangers* running diagonally across the front of their uniforms.

By the Numbers

 The Rangers have had a lot of success on the ice. Here are just a few interesting facts:

The Rangers have won four Stanley Cup championships: 1928, 1933, 1940, and 1994.

4

The Rangers have appeared in the Stanley Cup Final 11 times.

11

The Rangers have appeared in the playoffs 63 times.

63

"The Great One," Wayne Gretzky, played for the Rangers for three seasons from 1996 until 1999.
3

Coach Mike Keenan and Rangers players celebrate their 1994 Stanley Cup win. ▶

Madison Square Garden is the oldest sports facility in the New York area.

Game Night

The Rangers play all of their home games at Madison Square Garden (MSG) in New York, New York. They share the arena with basketball's New York Knicks. MSG can seat more than 18,000 fans for hockey games. A $1 billion renovation was completed in 2013. The most unique feature of MSG is the ceiling. It is concave—that means it is curved inward like the inside of a bowl. And the ceiling is supported by steel cables, not columns. This allows for great views from any seat.

We're Famous

The New York Rangers have been featured in several TV shows, especially those set in New York City. The popular sitcom *Friends* featured a character getting hit in the face by a hockey puck at a Rangers game. In the episode, the characters wear Rangers gear and hold up a huge Rangers foam finger. Footage from an actual game is shown, as well as the inside of MSG. The team's huge video screen is used to show the character holding his nose after the puck hits him.

Uniforms

HOME

AWAY

Mask as Art

While a goalie mask is used to protect a player's head and face from injury, many goalies use their masks to express themselves. Goalies are able to show their personalities and stand out from the rest of the team. The Rangers' Igor Shesterkin is one of the best goalies in the NHL. His custom goalie masks are unforgettable every season. Shesterkin's mask often includes the Statue of Liberty as a tribute to the city of New York. His mask also includes images of other iconic New York City buildings.

Truly Weird

At the age of 44 years, three months, and eight days, Lester Patrick played goalie for the Rangers during a 1928 Stanley Cup Final. Patrick was the Rangers' coach at the time. He made the decision to play when starting goalie Lorne Chabot was struck in the eye by a puck mid-game. At the time, teams rarely had a backup goalie. The other team's coach had to allow a substitute player, but their coach refused two of the Rangers' possible subs. So Patrick took matters into his own hands and suited up to play goalie for his team. He allowed only one goal on 19 shots and led the Rangers to an **overtime** victory.

Team Spirit

The New York Rangers are the only NHL team that does not have a mascot. The team feels a mascot would be a distraction to the players and fans. The Rangers want their fans to focus on the game and take it seriously. They also feel that their blue, red, and white jerseys and logo are iconic enough to identify the team without the help of a mascot. Rangers' fans are some of the most devoted and loudest in the NHL. They sing several chants throughout the game to keep the team motivated. A live organist plays during games to keep the crowd engaged. Fans are so important to the team that after a win, players gather at center ice to salute the crowd.

◀ **Based on yearly game attendance and social media followers, the Rangers have around 1.4 million fans.**

Heroes of History

Henrik Lundqvist
Goalie | 2005–2020

Nicknamed "King Hank," Henrik Lundqvist is the only goalie in NHL history to have 30 or more wins in each of his first seven seasons. Lundqvist spent his entire NHL career with the Rangers and joined the Hockey **Hall of Fame** in 2023. Although Lundqvist never won a Stanley Cup, he led the Rangers to the Stanley Cup Final in 2014. The Rangers retired Lundqvist's jersey the same day he announced his retirement from hockey in 2021. That means no player can wear the number 30 again.

Mark Messier
Center | 1991–1997 and 2000–2004

The Rangers nicknamed Mark Messier "The Messiah." This is another word for *savior,* and Messier saved the day for the Rangers many times. Messier played 10 seasons with the Rangers. He was the first and only player to captain two different Stanley Cup championship teams, the Edmonton Oilers and the New York Rangers. Messier is second all-time for career playoff points, with 295. He is also third all-time for regular-season games played, with 1,756. His 1,887 points rank third all-time.

Brian Leetch
Defenseman | 1987–2004

The Rangers knew Brian Leetch was a star not long into his **rookie** season. He scored 23 goals and had 48 **assists**. Leetch was the NHL Rookie of the Year in the 1988–1989 season. He is one of only six defensemen in NHL history to record more than 100 points in a season and one of eight to earn more than 1,000 points in his career. Leetch was the top scorer in the 1993–1994 playoffs. That season, he led the Rangers to their first Stanley Cup in over 50 years. Leetch played in nine NHL **All-Star** games.

Rod Gilbert
Right Wing | 1960–1978

Rod Gilbert (zhil-BEHR) spent his entire career with the Rangers. He scored 1,021 points, including 406 goals, which are the most in team history. Gilbert set the record with 615 assists, an accomplishment eventually passed by Brian Leetch, with 741. Gilbert had a lasting effect on the Rangers both on and off the ice. The Mr. Ranger Award was created in the 2021–2022 season to honor Gilbert. This award recognizes the Rangers player who honors Gilbert's legacy by displaying leadership qualities as a player and member of the community.

Big Days

1979

In 1979, the Rangers beat the division-leading New York Islanders to reach the Stanley Cup Final. They lose to the Montreal Canadiens and will not make the Finals for another 15 years.

Stéphane Matteau's double overtime game-winning goal is one of the best moments in Rangers history. The win sends the Rangers to the Stanley Cup Final.

1994

1994

The Rangers break a 54-year curse and win the Stanley Cup, establishing Mark Messier, Brian Leetch, and Mike Richter as some of the best-loved players in team history.

Down three games to two in the first round of the 2013 playoffs, the Rangers need two wins to advance, and goalie Henrik Lundqvist delivers. He has back-to-back **shutouts** and stops 62 shots. The Rangers move on to the second round.

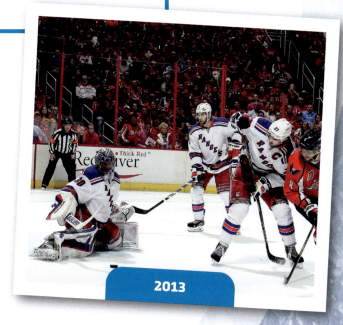

2013

Modern-Day Marvels

Artemi Panarin
Left Wing | 2019–Present

Artemi Panarin began his career playing in the Kontinental Hockey League in his home country of Russia. In 2015, he moved to the United States and joined the Chicago Blackhawks. Panarin's first NHL goal and **hat trick** were against the New York Rangers. Four years later in 2019, Panarin joined the Rangers. Panarin began the 2023–2024 season with a 15-game point streak—10 goals and 16 assists—to set a Rangers record for the longest run to open a season.

Vincent Trocheck
Center | 2022–Present

Vincent Trocheck played for the Florida Panthers and the Carolina Hurricanes before joining the Rangers in 2022. He scored 47 goals in his first two seasons with the Rangers. He is a leader and a complete player, which means he is good at offense, defense, and **power plays**. Trocheck was named an NHL All-Star for the second time in 2024. Trocheck has scored 30 game-winning goals in his career as of December 2024.

Igor Shesterkin
Goalie | 2019–Present

The Rangers selected Igor Shesterkin in the fourth round of the 2014 NHL Draft. But he played hockey in Russia for five years to improve his skills before playing in the NHL. Goalies don't often get assists, but Shesterkin became the first goalie in NHL history to have two assists in a playoff game when his team faced being eliminated from the playoffs. Shesterkin won the 2021–2022 Vezina Trophy as the best goalie in the NHL.

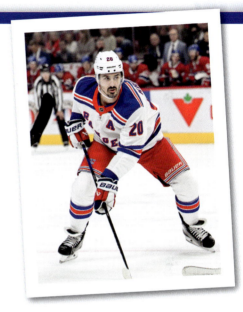

Chris Kreider
Left Wing | 2012–Present

Kreider made his NHL debut during the 2012 playoffs, just a few weeks after his college hockey career was finished. Kreider helped the team to the Eastern Conference Final that season. He holds the unique record of scoring the most playoff goals before playing his first NHL regular-season game. Kreider has scored more than 300 career goals, all with the New York Rangers.

Mike Richter was named the NHL's most outstanding player in 1994, an honor voted on by other players in the league.

The G.O.A.T.

Mike Richter played for the Rangers from 1989 until 2003. A three-time NHL All-Star, Richter played goalie for the Rangers for his whole 14-year career. He was the starting goalie during the Rangers' memorable run for the Stanley Cup championship in 1994, breaking a 54-year drought. Richter ranks second in team history in wins and is tied for fifth in shutouts. Richter also led the US men's hockey team to a silver medal in the 2002 Olympic Games. The Rangers retired his number 35 jersey in 2004.

Fan Favorite

Harry Howell spent 17 seasons of his 21-year career with the New York Rangers. He was well-loved for his calm attitude and leadership abilities. Howell was a defenseman whose biggest strength wasn't his toughness, but his knowledge of the game. During the 1964–1965 season, Howell was named an assistant coach even though he was still an active player. Howell was added to the Hockey Hall of Fame in 1979. The Rangers retired his number 3 jersey in 2009.

The Big Game

In the 1994 playoffs, a series between the Rangers and the New Jersey Devils produced one of the biggest moments in history, not only for the Rangers, but also for the entire NHL. The Rangers were down three games to two and faced a tough Game 6 in New Jersey. Rangers' captain Mark Messier told reporters before the game that he could promise a Rangers victory. At the end of the second period, the Rangers were losing by one. It looked like Messier would not be keeping his promise. But in the third period, with his back against the wall, Messier tied the game. With time running out, Messier once again put the puck in the net for another career hat trick and a victory for the Rangers. Messier had kept his promise!

Mark Messier's big promise during the 1994 playoffs took the Rangers all the way to a Stanley Cup win— one of the greatest moments in team history. ▶

The Rangers drafted Chris Kreider in 2009, but he finished his college hockey career at Boston College before joining the team in 2012.

Amazing Feats

Penalty Minutes

In 1989–1990, Troy Mallette racked up 305 penalty minutes (PIM), the most for a Ranger in a single season.

305

Shutouts

Goalie John Ross Roach set a Rangers record in 1928–1929 when he logged 13 shutouts.

13

Points

In addition to keeping the puck out of the net, defenseman Brian Leetch was also good at scoring. He holds the Rangers' record for most points by a defenseman in a season with 102, set in 1991–1992.

102

Power Play Goals

Power plays are a key to winning in the NHL. In 2021–2022, Chris Kreider led the Rangers with 26 power play goals.

26

All-Time Best

MOST POINTS

1	Rod Gilbert	1,021
2.	Brian Leetch	981
3.	Jean Ratelle	817
4.	Andy Bathgate	729
5.	Mark Messier	691

MOST GOALS

1	Rod Gilbert	406
2.	Jean Ratelle	336
3.	Chris Kreider	309
4.	Adam Graves	280
5.	Andy Bathgate	272

MOST ASSISTS

1	Brian Leetch	741
2.	Rod Gilbert	615
3.	Jean Ratelle	481
4.	Andy Bathgate	457
5.	Walt Tkaczuk	451

MOST WINS

1	Henrik Lundqvist	459
2.	Mike Richter	301
3.	Ed Giacomin	267
4.	Gump Worsley	204
5.	John Vanbiesbrouck	200

HIGHEST SAVE %

1	Igor Shesterkin*	.919
2.	Henrik Lundqvist	.918
3.	Gump Worsley	.913
4.	Alexandar Georgiev	.908
5.	Mike Dunham	.908
	Jacques Plante	.908

MOST HAT TRICKS

1	Bill Cook	9
2.	Rod Gilbert	7
3.	Mika Zibanejad	7
4.	Nine players tied	6

*stats accurate through December 2024

Rod Gilbert is the only player in Rangers history to score 400 or more career goals with the team. ▶

GLOSSARY

All-Star (ALL STAR) An All-Star is a player chosen as one of the best in their sport.

assist (uh-SIST) An assist is a play that helps a teammate score a goal.

division (dih-VIZSH-un) A division is a group of teams within the NHL that compete with each other to have the best record each season and advance to the playoffs.

draft (DRAFT) A draft is a yearly event when teams take turns choosing new players. In the NHL, teams can select North American players between the ages of 18 and 20, and players from outside North America between the ages of 18 and 21.

expansion team (ex-SPAHN-shun TEEM) An expansion team is a new team that is formed when the league expands its membership.

Hall of Fame (HAHL of FAYM) The Hockey Hall of Fame is a museum in Ontario, Canada. The best players and coaches in the game are honored there.

hat trick (HAT TRIK) A hat trick occurs when one player scores three goals in a single game.

overtime (OH-vur-tym) Overtime is extra time added to the end of a game when the regular time is up and the score is tied.

playoffs (PLAY-offs) Playoffs are games that take place after the end of the regular season to determine each year's championship team.

power play (POW-uhr PLAY) A power play occurs when a player gets a penalty and the other team has more players on the ice.

rival (RYE-vuhl) A rival is a team's top competitor, which they try to outdo and play better than each season.

rookie (ROOK-ee) A rookie is a new or first-year player in a professional sport.

shutout (SHUT-owt) A shutout occurs when a goalie keeps the other team from scoring any goals.

FAST FACTS

- The first indoor hockey game was in 1875 in Montreal, Quebec.

- The Rangers were the first NHL team to travel by plane. In 1929, the team flew to Toronto to play the Maple Leafs.

- The Rangers' biggest **rival** is the New Jersey Devils. The teams' home arenas are only separated by 14 miles (22.5 kilometers) across the Hudson River.

- The Rangers are the second highest-valued NHL team. They are worth $2 billion.

ONE STRIDE FURTHER

- What makes someone remain a loyal fan to a team when they go more than 50 years without a championship? Many fans are devoted to their teams for their entire lives. How does a fan hold on to hope that the team will eventually turn things around and achieve success?

- Most sports teams have a mascot. Why do you think the Rangers believe a mascot would be a distraction for their fans? List the pros and cons of having a mascot.

- Based on what you read in this book, what do you think it takes for a team to win a major championship? Good players? A strong fan base? Something else? Discuss your ideas with a friend.

- Ask friends and family members to name their favorite sport to watch and their favorite sport to play. Keep track and make a graph to see which sports are the most popular.

FIND OUT MORE

IN THE LIBRARY

Creamer, Chris and Todd Radom. *Fabric of the Game: The Stories Behind the NHL's Names, Logos, and Uniforms.* New York: Skyhorse Sports Publishing, 2020.

Davidson, B. Keith. *NHL.* New York, NY: Crabtree, 2022.

Laughlin, Kara L. *Hockey.* Parker, CO: The Child's World, 2024.

Olson, Ethan. *Great NHL Stanley Cup Championships.* San Diego, CA: BrightPoint Press, 2024.

ON THE WEB

Visit our website for links about the New York Rangers:
childsworld.com/links

Note to Parents, Caregivers, Teachers, and Librarians: We routinely verify our web links to make sure they are safe and active sites. So encourage your readers to check them out!

INDEX